WORLD WINDOWS
Ways to Travel

HEINLE
CENGAGE Learning™

YSG
A YBM COMPANY
Young & Son
Global, Inc.

How do you get to school?

Contents

ship

sailboat

airplane

helicopter

car

train

People travel on land by car.

People travel on land by train.

People travel on water
by ship.

People travel on water
by sailboat.

9

People travel in the air
by airplane.

People travel in the air
by helicopter.

11

bicycle

bus

People travel every day.

balloon

canoe

People get from place to place in many ways.

How do people travel?

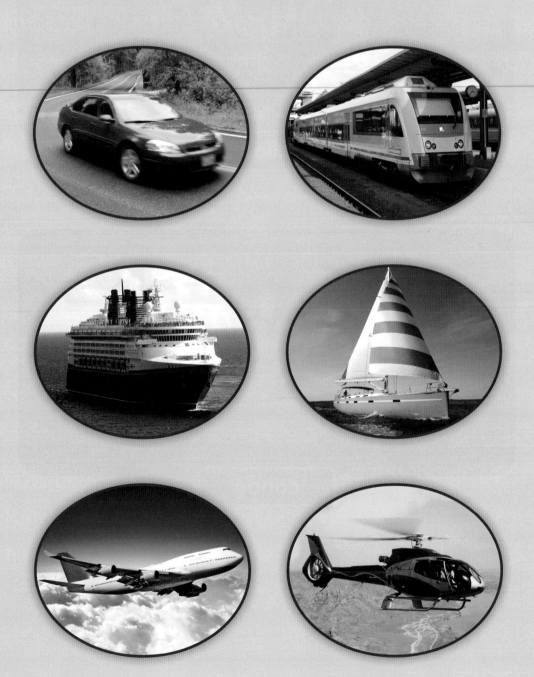

Watch It Go!

Watch the car go by land,
Go by land, go by land.
Watch the car go by land,
To get from place to place!

Watch the ship go by water,
Go by water, go by water.
Watch the ship go by water,
To get from place to place!

Watch the airplane go by air,
Go by air, go by air.
Watch the airplane go by air,
To get from place to place!

Index